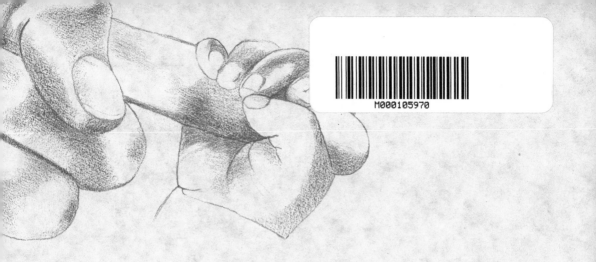

I look into his calm blue eyes, which are seeing life for the first time. Once again, so are mine.

—MARK GERZON
Contemporary American writer

FATHERHOOD

The family you come from isn't as important as the family you're going to have.

—RING LARDNER (1885-1933)
American writer

No man can possibly know what life means, what the world means, what anything means, until he has a child and loves it. And then the whole universe changes and nothing will ever again seem exactly as it seemed before.

—LAFCADIO HEARN (1850-1904)
Greek-born American writer

In a bleary tradition, I awoke to my first full day
as a father with a hangover.

—MIKE CLARY
Contemporary American writer

Do engine drivers, I wonder, eternally wish
they were small boys?

—BRIAN O'NOLAN (1910-1966)
Irish writer

Just one way, you do get back home. You have a boy or a girl of your own and now and then you remember, and you know how they feel, and it's almost the same thing as if you were your own self again, as young as you could remember.

—JAMES AGEE (1909-1955)
American writer

The best way to make children is to make them happy.
—OSCAR WILDE (1854-1900)
Irish writer

Everyone calls his son his son, whether he has talents or has not talents.

—CONFUCIUS (551-497 B.C.)
Chinese philosopher

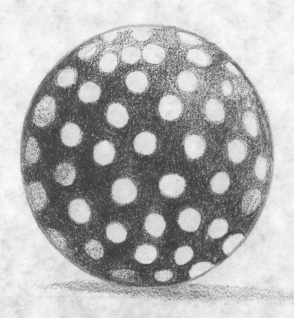

Parenthood remains the greatest single
preserve of the amateur.
—ALVIN TOFFLER, b. 1928
Contemporary American writer

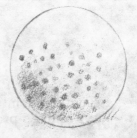

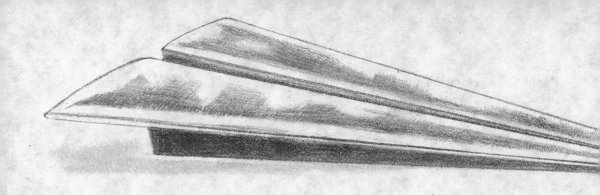

I could not point to any need in childhood as strong as that for a father's protection.

—SIGMUND FREUD (1856-1939)
Austrian; founder of psychoanalysis

I like it to be known that, yes, I looked after the baby. . . and I am proud of it.

—JOHN LENNON (1940-1980)
English singer and songwriter

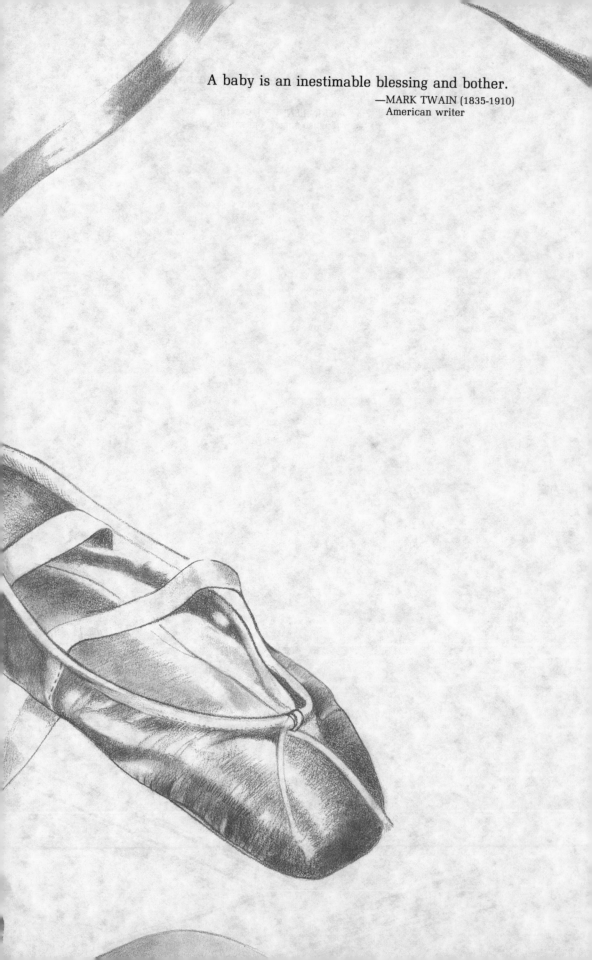

A baby is an inestimable blessing and bother.
—MARK TWAIN (1835-1910)
American writer

If I had children now, I should send them to the ballet. At any
rate it is better than the university. Their feet alone might be
spoiled in the ballet, but at the university it is their heads.

—LEO TOLSTOY (1828-1910)
Russian writer

Some parents. . . say it is toy guns that make boys warlike. . . but give a boy a rubber duck and he will seize its neck like the butt of a pistol and shout "Bang!"

—GEORGE F. WILL, b. 1941
American writer

The time not to become a father is
eighteen years before a war.
—E.B. WHITE (1899-1985)
American writer

There ought not be any doubt that children should be fed on fairy tales as their souls' most natural food.

—HAVELOCK ELLIS (1859-1939)
English scientist and writer

Adolescence is that period in a kid's life when his or her parents become more difficult.

—RYAN O'NEAL, b. 1941
American actor

Children rarely want to know who their parents were before they were parents. . .

—RUSSELL BAKER, b. 1925
American writer

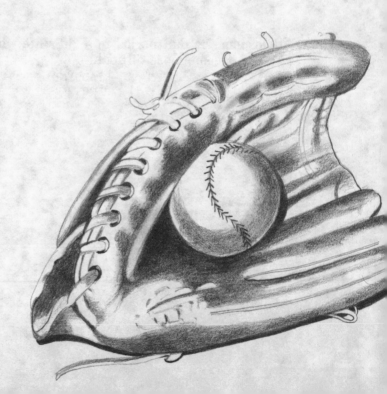

If you've never seen a real, fully developed look of disgust, just tell your son how you conducted yourself when you were a boy.

—KIN HUBBARD (1868-1930)
American humorist

The most ferocious animals are disarmed by caresses to their young.

—VICTOR HUGO (1802-1885)
French writer

Every child is born a genius.
—R. BUCKMINSTER FULLER (1895-1983)
American architect

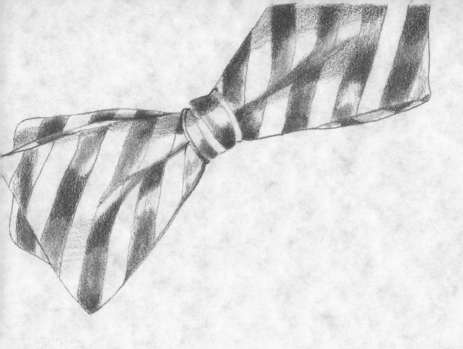

... the hardest truth for a father to learn: that his children are continuously growing up and moving away from him ... Such growing is especially bittersweet with a daughter because you are always in love with her.

—BILL COSBY, b. 1937
American entertainer

I do not love him because he is good, but because
he is my little child.

—RABINDRANATH TAGORE (1861-1941)
Indian poet

Happy is the father whose child finds his attempts to amuse it amusing.

—ROBERT LYND (1879-1949)
Irish journalist

The fundamental defect of fathers is that they want their children to be a credit to them.

—BERTRAND RUSSELL (1872-1970)
English mathematician and philosopher

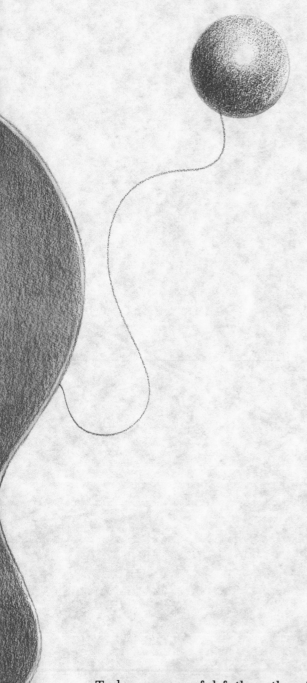

To be a successful father, there's one absolute rule: when you have a kid, don't look at it for the first two years.

—ERNEST HEMINGWAY (1899-1961)
American writer

The best brought-up children are those who have seen their parents as they are. Hypocrisy is not the parents' first duty.

—GEORGE BERNARD SHAW (1856-1950)
British playwright

. . . it is much less lonely sleeping when you can hear children breathing when you wake in the night.

—ERNEST HEMINGWAY (1899-1961)
American writer

. . . I love him so much that I hug him. . .and at night if I remember his tears I want to go into his room and hold his fat, sweaty hand that lies on the coverlet clutching some such treasure as an empty reel.

—SEÁN O'FAOLÁIN, b. 1900
Irish writer and educator

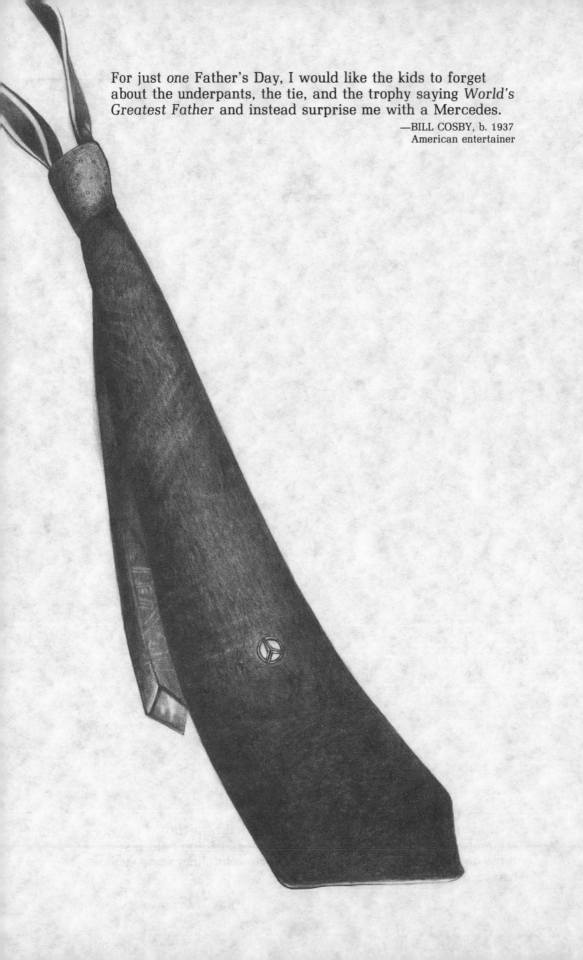

For just *one* Father's Day, I would like the kids to forget about the underpants, the tie, and the trophy saying *World's Greatest Father* and instead surprise me with a Mercedes.

—BILL COSBY, b. 1937
American entertainer

Charles knows so much about babies—he can have the
next one.

—DIANA, PRINCESS OF WALES, b. 1961

Our three young children are all in Switzerland, the older boy in Munich, and my wife and I are like middle-aged omnibus horses let loose in a pasture. The first time we have had a holiday together for 15 years; I feel like a barrel without hoops!

—WILLIAM JAMES (1842-1910)
American philosopher and educator

We've had bad luck with our kids—they've all grown up.
—CHRISTOPHER MORLEY (1890-1957)
American writer

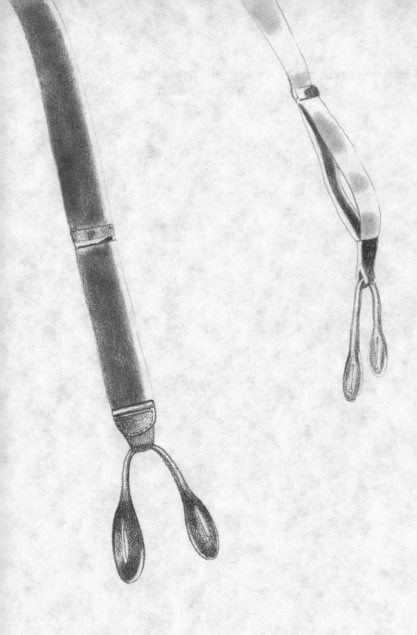

Women say. . . that if men had to have babies there soon
would be no babies in the world . . . I have sometimes wished
that some clever man would actually have a baby in a new,
labour-saving way; then all men could take it up, and one of
the oldest taunts in the world would be stilled forever.

—ROBERTSON DAVIES, b. 1913
Canadian writer

One word of command from me is obeyed by millions. . . but I cannot get my three daughters. . . to come down to breakfast on time.

—VISCOUNT ARCHIBALD WAVELL (1883-1950)
British army officer

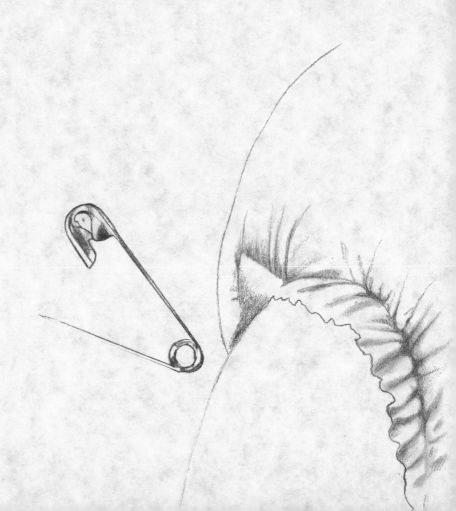

Money brings everything to you, even your daughters.

—HONORÉ DE BALZAC (1799-1850)
French writer

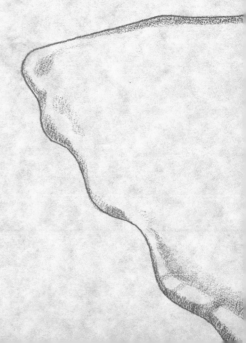

Raising kids is part joy and part guerilla warfare.
—EDWARD ASNER, b. 1929
American actor

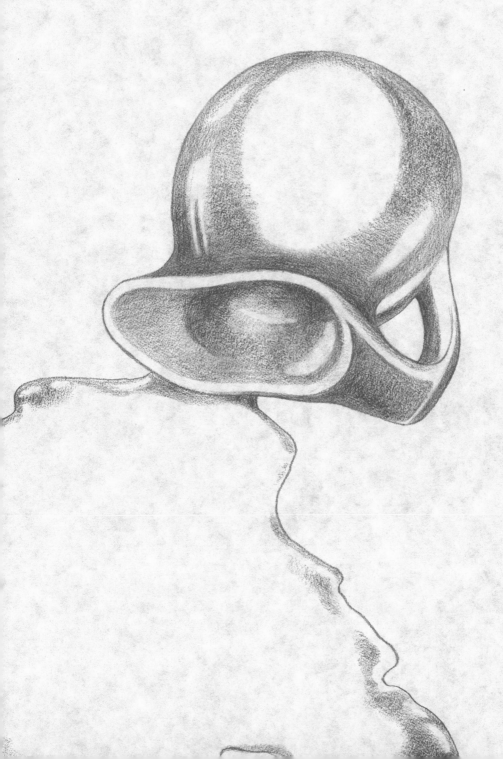

My fondest and earliest memory of my father is being able to get in his lap and sit. I still to this day sit in his lap, and he loves it. I don't think you're ever too old for that.

—HOLLY HESTON, b. 1961
Daughter of American actor Charlton Heston

For our part we have never understood the fear of some parents about babies getting mixed up in the hospital. What difference does it make so long as you get a good one?

—HEYWOOD BROUN (1888-1939)
American writer

You don't have to deserve your mother's love. You have to deserve your father's. He's more particular.

—ROBERT FROST (1874-1963)
American poet

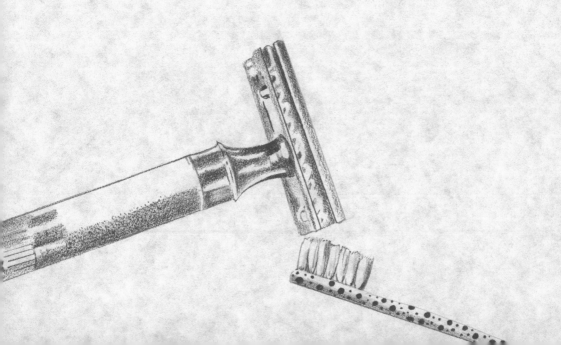

There are to us no ties at all just in being a father. A son is distinctly an acquired taste. It's the practice of parenthood that makes you feel that, after all, there may be something in it.

—HEYWOOD BROUN (1888-1939)
American writer

Wealth and children are the adornment of life.
—*THE KORAN*

I love these little people; and it is not a slight thing, when
they, who are so fresh from God, love us.

—CHARLES DICKENS (1812-1870)
English writer

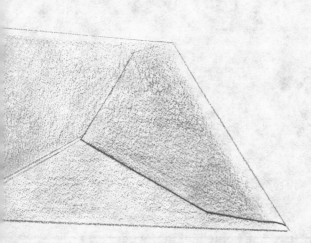

The most important thing a father can do for his children is to love their mother.

—REV. THEODORE HESBURGH, b. 1917
American Roman Catholic
clergyman and educator

There are one hundred and fifty-two distinctly different ways
of holding a baby—and all are right.
                    —HEYWOOD BROUN (1888-1939)
                      American writer

A man can deceive his fiancée or his mistress as much as he likes, and, in the eyes of a woman he loves, an ass may pass for a philosopher; but a daughter is a different matter.

—ANTON CHEKOV (1860-1904)
Russian writer

I believe children are handwrought.
—OSSIE DAVIS, b. 1917
American actor

Respect the child. Be not too much his parent. Trespass not
on his solitude.

—RALPH WALDO EMERSON (1803-1882)
American writer

Don't let yourself forget what it's like to be sixteen.
—ANONYMOUS

I doubt that *any* father has ever liked the music his children did.

—BILL COSBY, b. 1937
American entertainer

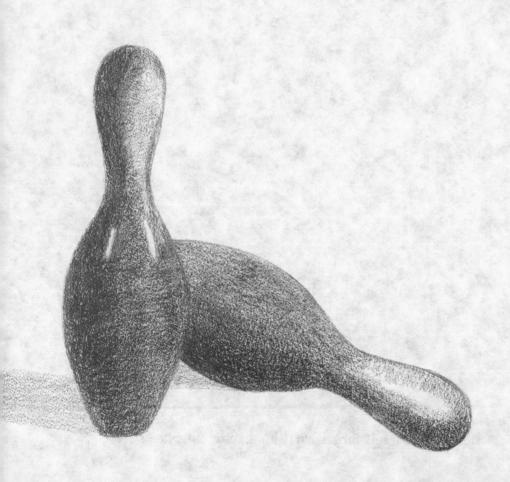

Having a family is like having a bowling alley installed in your brain.

—MARTIN MULL, b. 1943
American entertainer

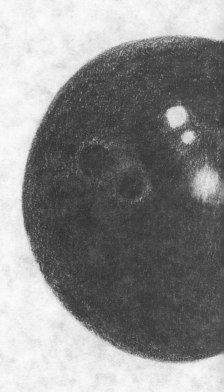

I have found the best way to give advice to your children is to
find out what they want and then advise them to do it.

—HARRY S TRUMAN (1844-1972)
33rd U.S. President

It is not enough for parents to understand children. They must accord children the privilege of understanding them.

—MILTON SAPIRSTEIN, b. 1914
American psychiatrist and writer

A child thinks twenty shillings and
twenty years can scarce ever be spent.

—BENJAMIN FRANKLIN (1706-1790)
American statesman, scientist,
and philosopher

It usually begins with the arrival at your bedside of a small child announcing, "I can't sleep"... you'd like to tell him to take a Junior Valium and go back to his room, but few parents can resist the moving pleas of a small child at night.

—RALPH SCHOENSTEIN, b. 1933
American writer

The hardest job kids face today is learning good manners without seeing any.

—FRED ASTAIRE (1899-1987)
American entertainer

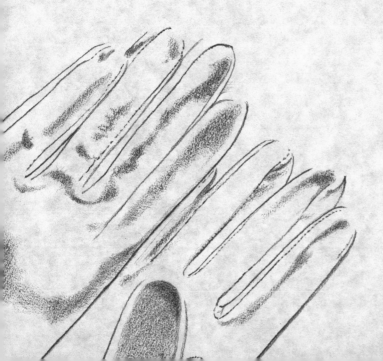

Never teach your child to be cunning, for you may be certain you will be one of the very first victims of his shrewdness.

—JOSH BILLINGS (1818-1885)
American humorist

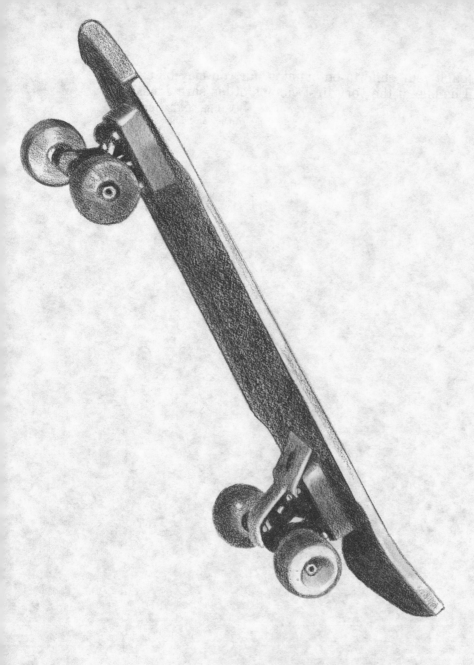

A father must never say, "Get those kids out of here; I'm trying to watch TV." If he does start saying this, he is liable to see one of his kids on the six o'clock news.

—BILL COSBY, b. 1937
American entertainer

"From the day your baby is born," counseled a famous
scholar, "you must teach him to do without things. Children
today love luxury too much. They have execrable manners,
flaunt authority, have no respect for their elders. . . What
kind of awful creatures will they be when they grow up?"
The scholar who wrote these words, incidentally, was
Socrates. . . in 399 B.C.

—BENNETT CERF (1898-1971)
American publisher

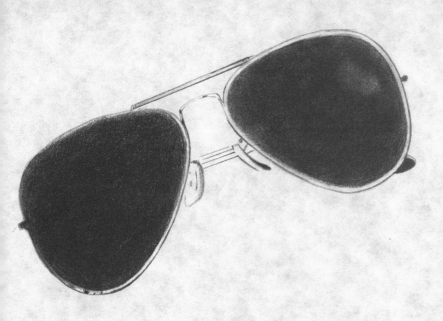

When men abandon the upbringing of their children to their wives, a loss is suffered by everyone, but perhaps most of all by themselves. For what they lose is the possibility of growth in themselves for being human which the stimulation of bringing up one's children gives.

—ASHLEY MONTAGU, b. 1905
American anthropologist

. . . when you have children of your own, you only then discover what fun they can be.

—CHARLES, PRINCE OF WALES, b. 1948

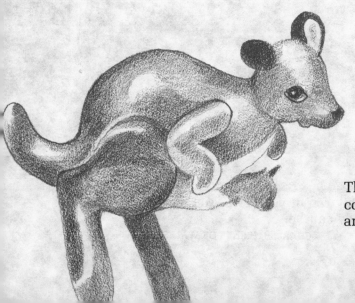

The age of a child is inversely correlated with the size of animals it prefers.

—DESMOND MORRIS, b. 1928
English anthropologist

If children grew up according to early indications, we should
have nothing but geniuses.

—JOHANN WOLFGANG VON GOETHE (1749-1832)
German writer

Men love their children, not because they are promising
plants, but because they are theirs.
—CHARLES MONTAGU, EARL OF HALIFAX (1661-1715)
English statesman

A child tells in the street what its father and mother say at home.

—THE TALMUD

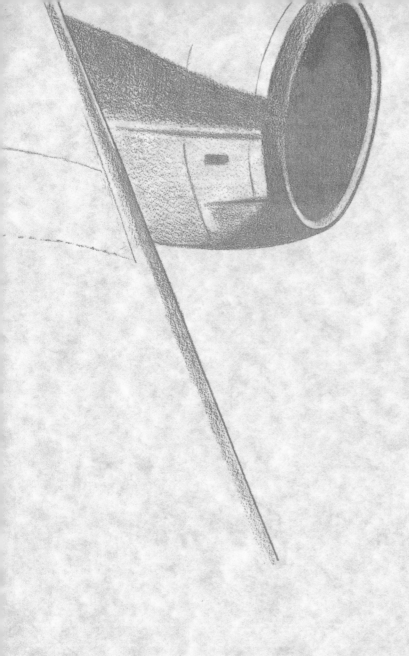

If you must hold yourself up to your child as an object lesson, hold yourself up as a warning and not as an example.

—GEORGE BERNARD SHAW (1856-1950)
British playwright

Most American children suffer too much mother
and too little father.

—GLORIA STEINEM, b. 1934
American writer and editor

If Father sees. . . his children as burdens, they will be burdens and if he sees his children as good; they will be good.

—WILLIAM REYNOLDS, b. 1928
American writer

My daddy doesn't work, he just goes to the office; but
sometimes he does errands on the way home.
                                    —ANONYMOUS

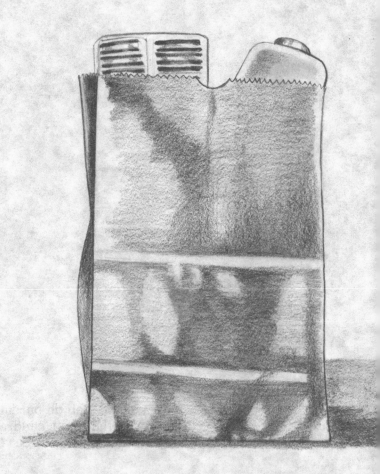

Oh, what a tangled web do parents weave
When they think that their children are naïve.

—BENNETT CERF (1898-1971)
American publisher

A man wants to protect his son, wants to teach him the things he, the father, has learned or thinks he has learned. But it's exactly that which a child resents.

—WILLIAM CARLOS WILLIAMS (1883-1963)
American physician and poet

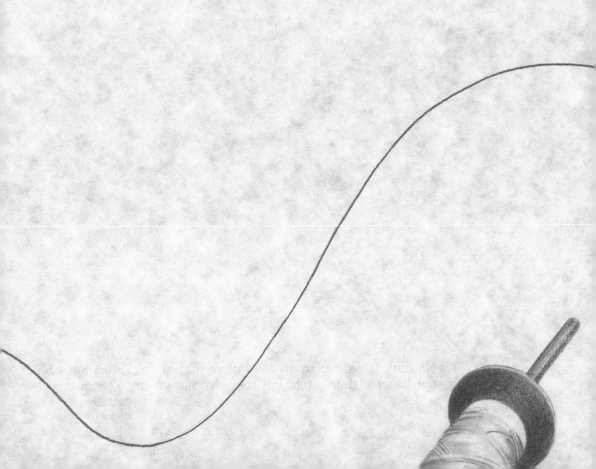

 Nothing is dearer to an old father than a daughter. Sons have spirits of higher pitch, but they are not given to fondness.

—EURIPIDES (c. 484-406 B.C.)
Greek playwright

Everyone is allowed to tell one lie in their lives. Don't waste it on chocolates. (Advice given to his daughter, Pamela, who had lied about stealing candy.)

—LORD L. MOUNTBATTEN (1900-1979)
British naval commander and statesman

Man is probably the only animal which even attempts to have anything to do with his half-grown children.

—GEORGE ROSS WELLS (1884-1962)
Canadian-born American writer

When a man lives in a house by himself he gets very precise habits and they get to be a pleasure. But it felt good to have some of them broken up. He knew he would have his habits again long after he would no longer have the boys.

—ERNEST HEMINGWAY (1899-1961)
American writer

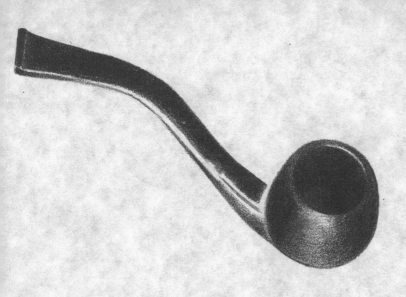

Only a person extraordinarily satisfied with himself can derive pleasure if this child in his house is a little person who gives him back nothing but reflection. You want a new story and not the old one, which wasn't particularly satisfactory in the first place.

—HEYWOOD BROUN (1888-1939)
American writer

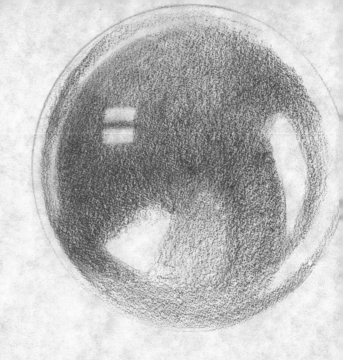

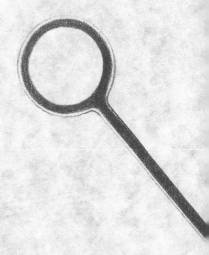

Pretty much all the honest truthtelling there is in the world is done by children.

—OLIVER WENDELL HOLMES (1809-1894)
American writer and physician

What's done to children,
they will do to society.

—DR. KARL MENNINGER, b. 1893
American psychologist

How easily a father's tenderness is recalled, and how quickly a son's offenses vanish at the slightest word of repentance!

—MOLIÈRE (1622-1673)
French playwright

The need for a father is as crucial as the need for a son, and the search of each for the other—through all the days of one's life—exempts no one. Happy the man who finds both.

—MAX LERNER, b. 1902
American writer and educator

You don't raise heroes, you raise sons. And if you treat them like sons, they'll turn out to be heroes, even if it's just in your own eyes.

—WALTER SCHIRRA, SR.
Father of American astronaut
Walter Schirra, Jr.

Fathers are allowed to rest while the infant is in the hospital. . . but seldom afterward. . .
—LARRY McMURTRY, b. 1936
Contemporary American writer

To a young person, naps don't mean much; he casually takes
them in English class. But to a father, a nap is a basic need...

—BILL COSBY, b. 1937
American entertainer

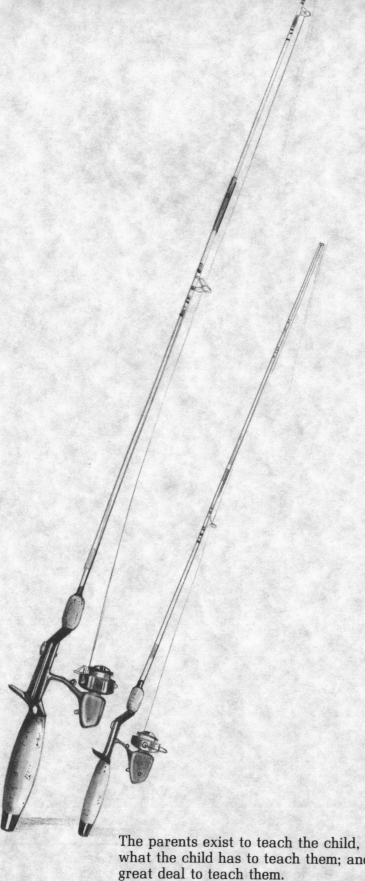

The parents exist to teach the child, but also they must learn
what the child has to teach them; and the child has a very
great deal to teach them.

—ARNOLD BENNETT (1867-1931)
English writer

I would rather see one of my children's faces kindle at the sight of the quay at Calais than be offered the chance of exploring by myself the Palaces of Peking.

—J.B. PRIESTLEY (1894-1984)
English writer

It is . . . sometimes easier to head an institute for the study of child guidance than it is to turn one brat into a decent human being.

—JOSEPH WOOD KRUTCH (1893-1970)
American writer and educator

One always knows that children have drawn a pretty fair hand if their father, when asked about his children, replies simply, with no superlative, no litany of accomplishments, "They're good kids."

—WILLIAM REYNOLDS, b. 1928
American writer

If the very old will remember, the very young will listen.

—CHIEF DAN GEORGE
Contemporary American actor

The world talks to the mind. Parents speak more intimately—
they talk to the heart.

—DR. HAIM G. GINOTT (1922-1973)
American writer and psychologist

The hardest part of raising children is teaching them to ride bicycles. . . A shaky child on a bicycle for the first time needs both support and freedom. The realization that this is what the child will always need can hit hard.

—SLOAN WILSON, b. 1920
Contemporary American writer

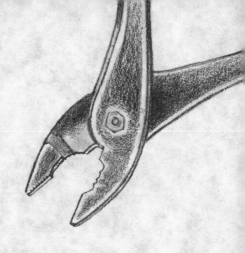

When I was a boy of fourteen, my father was so ignorant I
could hardly stand to have the old man around. But when I
got to be twenty-one, I was astonished at how much he had
learned in seven years.

—MARK TWAIN (1835-1910)
American writer

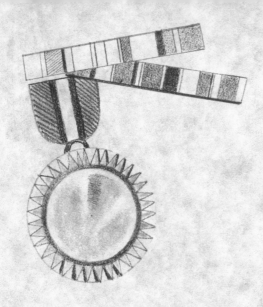

By profession I am a soldier and take pride in that fact. But I am prouder—infinitely prouder—to be a father.

—GEN. DOUGLAS MacARTHUR (1880-1964)
U.S. Army officer

It is not flesh and blood but the heart which makes us fathers
and sons.

—FRIEDRICH VON SCHILLER (1759-1805)
German writer and critic

There are only two lasting bequests we can hope to give our children. One of these is roots, the other, wings.

—HODDING CARTER (1907-1972)
American writer